I0762511

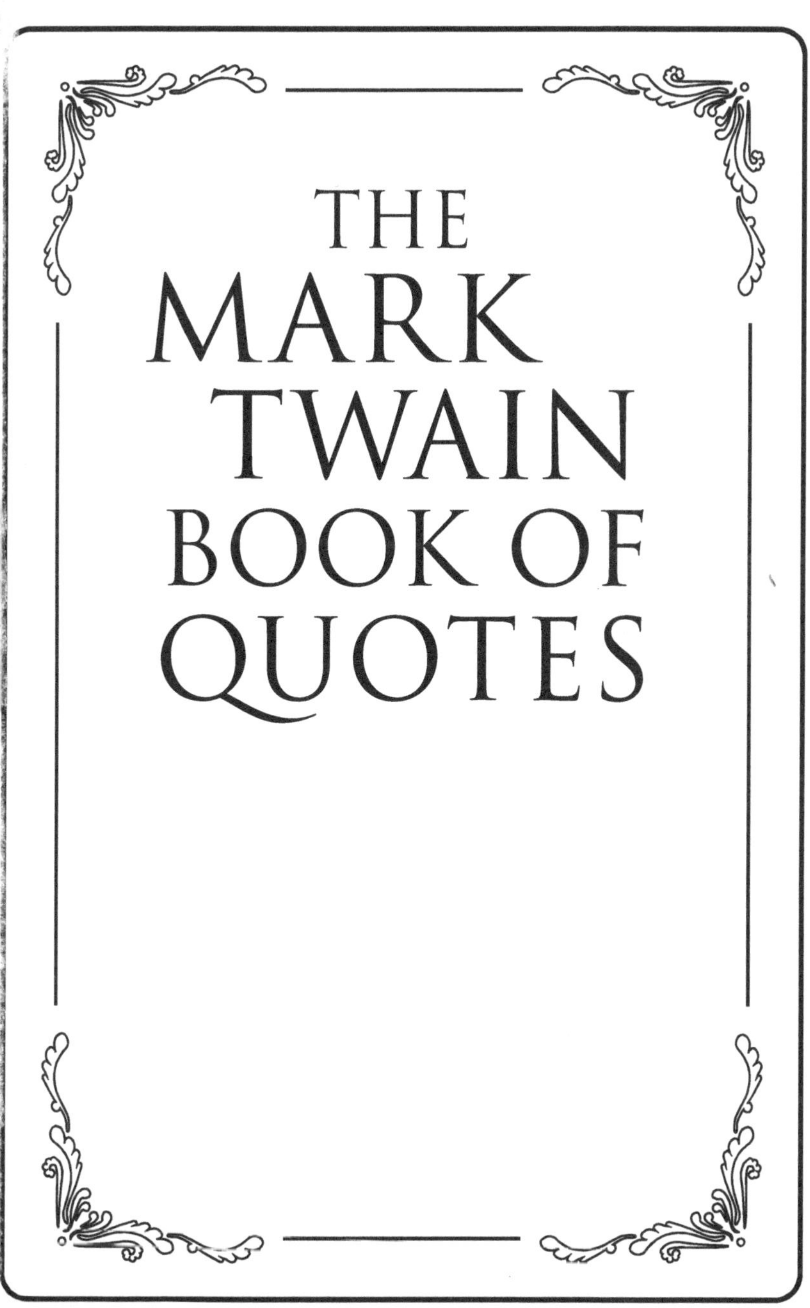

THE MARK TWAIN BOOK OF QUOTES

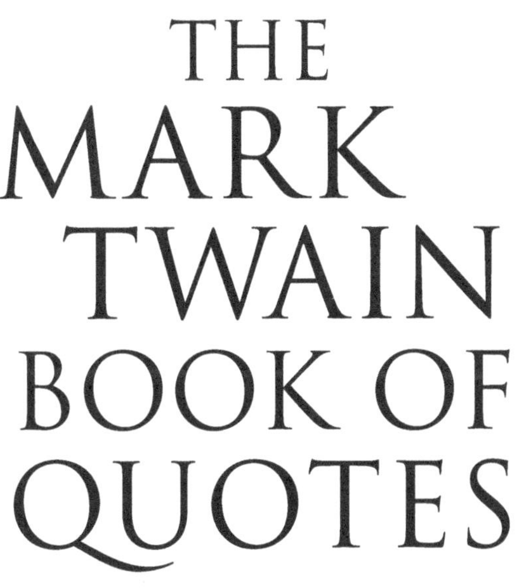

THE MARK TWAIN BOOK OF QUOTES

A COLLECTION OF SPEECHES, QUOTATIONS & ESSAYS FROM AMERICA'S GREATEST HUMORIST

EDITED BY TRAVIS HELLSTROM

Hatherleigh Press, Ltd.
62545 State Highway 10, Hobart, NY 13788, USA
hatherleighpress.com

THE MARK TWAIN BOOK OF QUOTES

Library of Congress Cataloging-in-Publication Data
is available.

ISBN: 978-1-961293-64-9

Interior and cover design by Carolyn Kasper

Printed in the United States

The authorized representative in the EU for product safety and compliance is Catarina Astrom, Blästorpsvägen 14, 276 35 Borrby, Sweden. info@hatherleighpress.com

10 9 8 7 6 5 4 3 2 1

Contents

Introduction vii

Truth & Lies 1

Education & Learning 13

Human Nature 27

Politics & Society 41

Religion & Philosophy 53

Humor & Writing 67

Life & Death 83

Travel & the World 97

Freedom & Independence 115

Quotes About Mark Twain 129

Important Moments in the Life of Mark Twain 139

Selected Writings & Memorable Moments 147

Advice to Youth 149

Mark Twain Meets Nikola Tesla 153

The War Prayer 157

Reflections on Mark Twain 163

INTRODUCTION

Mark Twain, born Samuel Langhorne Clemens in 1835, is perhaps America's most beloved literary icon. Known for his sharp wit, timeless wisdom, and irreverent humor, Twain spoke hard truths wrapped in laughter. His observations cut to the heart of human nature, society, and morality, offering a mirror that reflects as clearly today as it did more than a century ago.

Twain's books, including *The Adventures of Tom Sawyer, Adventures of Huckleberry Finn, A Connecticut Yankee in King Arthur's Court,* and *The Prince and the Pauper,* captured readers' imaginations and left a lasting mark on American literature. These stories didn't just entertain; they stirred conversation, challenged convention, and reshaped how America saw itself.

This book presents a collection of Twain's best quotations, organized thematically to inspire, challenge, and bring you laughter and a smile. Each quote is drawn from his speeches, letters, notebooks, and novels. It is my hope that this collection serves as a companion for you and a brief introduction to all the wonderful wisdom Mark Twain has to offer.

Against the assault of laughter,
nothing can stand.

—*The Mysterious Stranger* (1916)

RIVER LINE
RIVER LINE

Truth & Lies

Mark Twain believed that truth was not only stranger than fiction, but more difficult to tell and more essential to live by. He saw honesty as a rare courage and dishonesty as the favorite tool of fools and politicians. His sharp eye for human contradiction gave rise to observations that were not only humorous but piercingly honest. Twain's reflections on truth and lies still ring true today, speaking to our enduring struggle between candor and comfort, integrity and illusion.

If you tell the truth, you don't have to remember anything.

—Personal notebooks (1894)

Never let the truth get in the way of a good story.

—Often attributed

A lie can travel halfway around the world while the truth is putting on its shoes.

—Attributed (sometimes misattributed to Churchill)

Get your facts first, then you can distort them as you please.

—Quoted in Rudyard Kipling's *"From Sea to Sea"* (1899)

The truth is the most valuable thing we have. Let us economize it.

—*Following the Equator* (1897)

Whenever you are in doubt about what to do, just tell the truth. It will confound your enemies and astound your friends.

—Personal notebooks (date unknown)

There are three kinds of lies: lies, damned lies, and statistics.

—Often attributed to Twain, but sourced to Benjamin Disraeli

Truth is stranger than fiction, but it is because Fiction is obliged to stick to possibilities; Truth isn't.

—*Following the Equator* (1897)

I never could tell a lie that anybody would doubt, nor a truth that anybody would believe.

—Personal notebooks (date unknown)

It is better to deserve honors and not have them than to have them and not deserve them.

—Personal notebooks (1895)

A clear conscience is the sure sign of a bad memory.

—Often attributed

The man who tells the truth is never believed.

—Personal notebooks (early 1900s)

When in doubt, tell the truth.

—Personal notebooks (1905)

In religion and politics, people's beliefs and convictions are in almost every case gotten at second-hand, and without examination.

—*Autobiography of Mark Twain* (2010)

No real gentleman will tell the naked truth in the presence of ladies.

—Personal notebooks (1895)

It is curious that physical courage should be so common in the world and moral courage so rare.

—*Mark Twain in Eruption* (1940)

The truth has no defense against a fool determined to believe a lie.

—Quoted in multiple essays

Most people are bothered by those passages in Scripture which they cannot understand; but as for me, I always notice that the passages in Scripture which trouble me most are those which I do understand.

—Personal notebooks (1902)

The best liar is he who makes the smallest amount of lying go the longest way.

—Personal notebooks (date unknown)

A man is never more truthful than when he acknowledges himself a liar.

—Personal notebooks (1897)

RIVER LINE
RIVER LINE

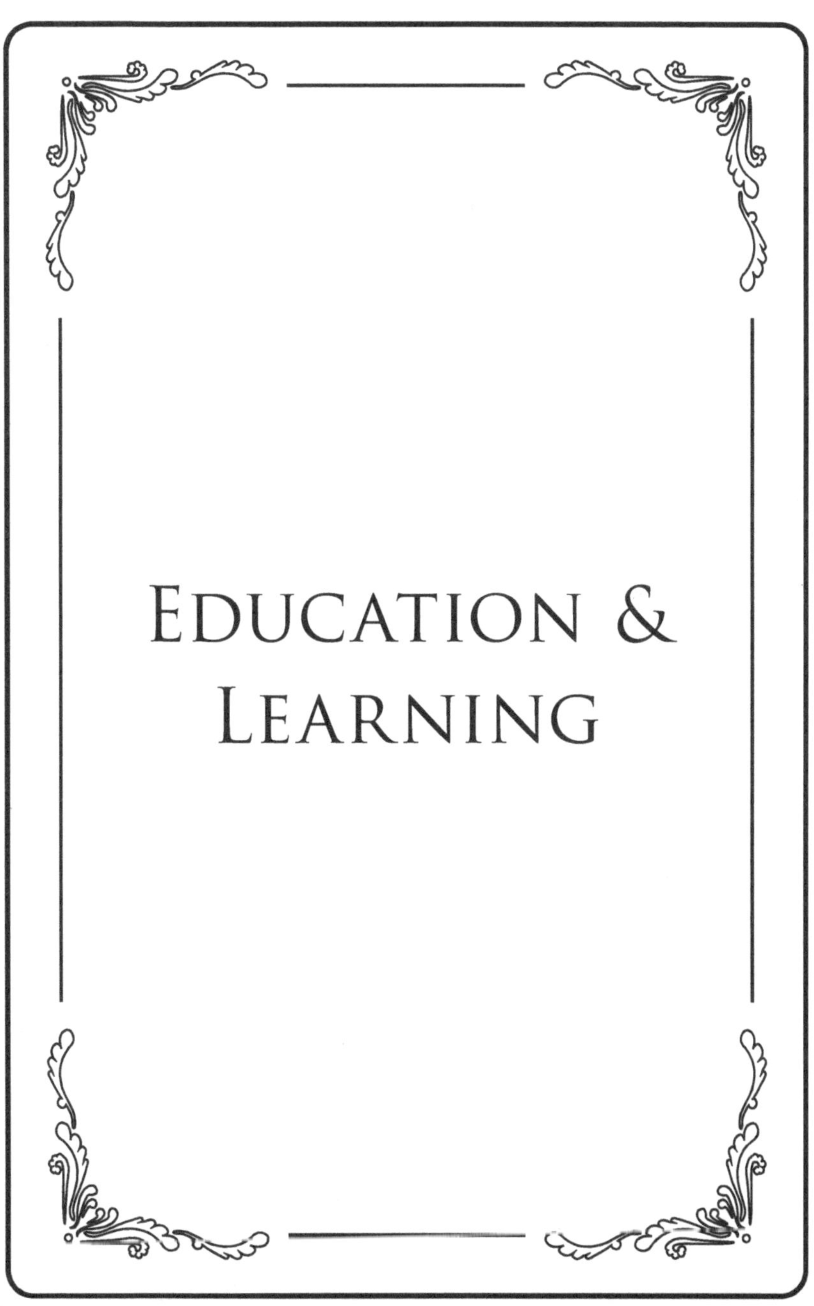

Education & Learning

Mark Twain cared deeply about learning, but he didn't put much stock in formal schooling. He valued curiosity, independent thought, and the kind of wisdom you gain from life. These quotes show how he saw education: something that should spark freedom, not squash it.

Every time you stop a school, you will have to build a jail. What you gain at one end you lose at the other. It's like feeding a dog on his own tail. It won't fatten the dog.

—Speech given in 1900

College ain't for everyone, and it wasn't for me, but libraries? Now those are for anyone.

—Personal notebooks (date unknown)

A successful book is not made of what is in it, but what is left out of it.

—Personal notebooks (1893)

The face of the water, in time, became a wonderful book... which told its mind to me without reserve.

—*Life on the Mississippi*, (1883)

Don't explain your author: it isn't nice to speak ill of the dead.

—Personal notebooks (date unknown)

A classic is a book which people praise and don't read.

—Personal notebooks (1900)

No man was ever great who had not a great mother—it is hardly an exaggeration to say that Lincoln's mother, in death, did more for him than she could have done in life.

—*The Wit and Wisdom of Mark Twain* (1998)

The man who reads too much and uses his own brain too little falls into lazy habits of thinking.

—Personal notebooks (date unknown)

A man should never neglect his family for business—or for school, if he can help it.

—Personal notebooks (date unknown)

Everything has its limit—even education.

—Personal notebooks (1894)

The best minds are not always found in the best schools. They're often too busy learning elsewhere.

—Personal notebooks (date unknown)

Education consists mainly in what we have unlearned.

—Personal notebooks (1898)

Training is everything. The peach was once a bitter almond; cauliflower is nothing but cabbage with a college education.

—*Pudd'nhead Wilson* (1894)

The educated man is not the man who can answer the questions, but the man who can ask them.

—Paraphrased

The man who does not read good books has no advantage over the man who can't read them.

—Often attributed

What a good thing Adam had. When he said a good thing he knew nobody had said it before.

—Personal notebooks (1898)

We have the best government that money can buy.

—Personal notebooks (1898)

I never let schooling interfere with my education.

—Personal notebooks (1905)

I was gratified to be able to answer promptly, and I did. I said I didn't know.

—*Life on the Mississippi* (1883)

Books are for people who wish they were somewhere else.

—Often attributed

The man who is a pessimist before 48 knows too much; if he is an optimist after it, he knows too little.

—Personal notebooks (date unknown)

I don't believe in colleges but I do believe in libraries.

—Speech excerpt

It is better to keep your mouth shut and appear stupid than to open it and remove all doubt.

—Often attributed

The man with a new idea is a crank until the idea succeeds.

—*Following the Equator* (1897)

Out of the public school grows the greatness of a nation.

—Speech excerpt

To learn to read is to light a fire; every syllable that is spelled out is a spark.

—Paraphrased

When you fish for love, bait with your heart, not your brain.

—Personal notebooks (1898)

RIVER LINE
RIVER LINE

Human Nature

Twain understood people—how generous and funny we can be, and how selfish and cruel, too. He paid attention to the way we act when no one is watching and wasn't afraid to call out what he saw. These quotes capture what it means to be human, in all our messy, complicated, and sometimes hilarious ways.

Man is the only animal that blushes. Or needs to.

—*Following the Equator* (1897)

The more I learn about people, the more I like my dog.

—Often attributed

Clothes make the man. Naked people have little or no influence in society.

—Personal notebooks (1893)

The human race has only one really effective weapon, and that is laughter.

—Albert Bigelow Paine's authorized biography of Mark Twain (1912)

Of all the animals, man is the only one that is cruel. He is the only one that inflicts pain for the pleasure of doing it.

—*The Damned Human Race* (1905)

The secret source of humor is not joy but sorrow; there is no humor in heaven.

—Quoted in *"Mark Twain and I"* by Helen Keller

The average American is a good-hearted, fair-minded, generous, hospitable, and honest person.

—Autobiographical dictation (1906)

Familiarity breeds contempt—and children.

—Personal notebooks (1894)

We are all alike, on the inside.

—Personal notebooks (1898)

Kindness is a language which the deaf can hear and the blind can see.

—Personal notebooks (1898)

Human beings can be awful cruel to one another.

—*The Adventures of Huckleberry Finn* (1885)

The worst loneliness is to not be comfortable with yourself.

—Personal notebooks (1898)

A man cannot be comfortable without his own approval.

—Personal notebooks (1906)

It is easier to stay out than get out.

—Personal notebooks (date unknown)

Nothing so needs reforming as other people's habits.

—*Pudd'nhead Wilson* (1894)

All men are liars; all women are liars too. Just not at the same time.

—Personal notebooks (date unknown)

The dog is a gentleman; I hope to go to his heaven, not man's.

—*Letter to W. D. Howells* (1899)

We are all fools in turn.

—Personal notebooks (date unknown)

Man was made at the end of the week's work, when God was tired.

—Personal notebooks (1903)

Be good and you will be lonesome.

—Personal notebooks (1903)

I can live for two months on a good compliment.

—Often attributed, (c. 1907)

Never argue with stupid people, they will drag you down to their level and then beat you with experience.

—Often attributed

Of all the things I've lost, I miss my mind the most.

—Often attributed

There are people who can do all fine and heroic things but one: keep from telling their happiness to the unhappy.

—Personal notebooks (1896)

The trouble ain't that there is too many fools, but that the lightning ain't distributed right.

—Personal notebooks (1894)

Always do right. This will gratify some people and astonish the rest.

—Letter to a young man (1901)

The universal brotherhood of man is our most precious possession.

—Speech given in 1906

Let us be thankful for the fools. But for them the rest of us could not succeed.

—Personal notebooks (1898)

RIVER LINE
RIVER LINE

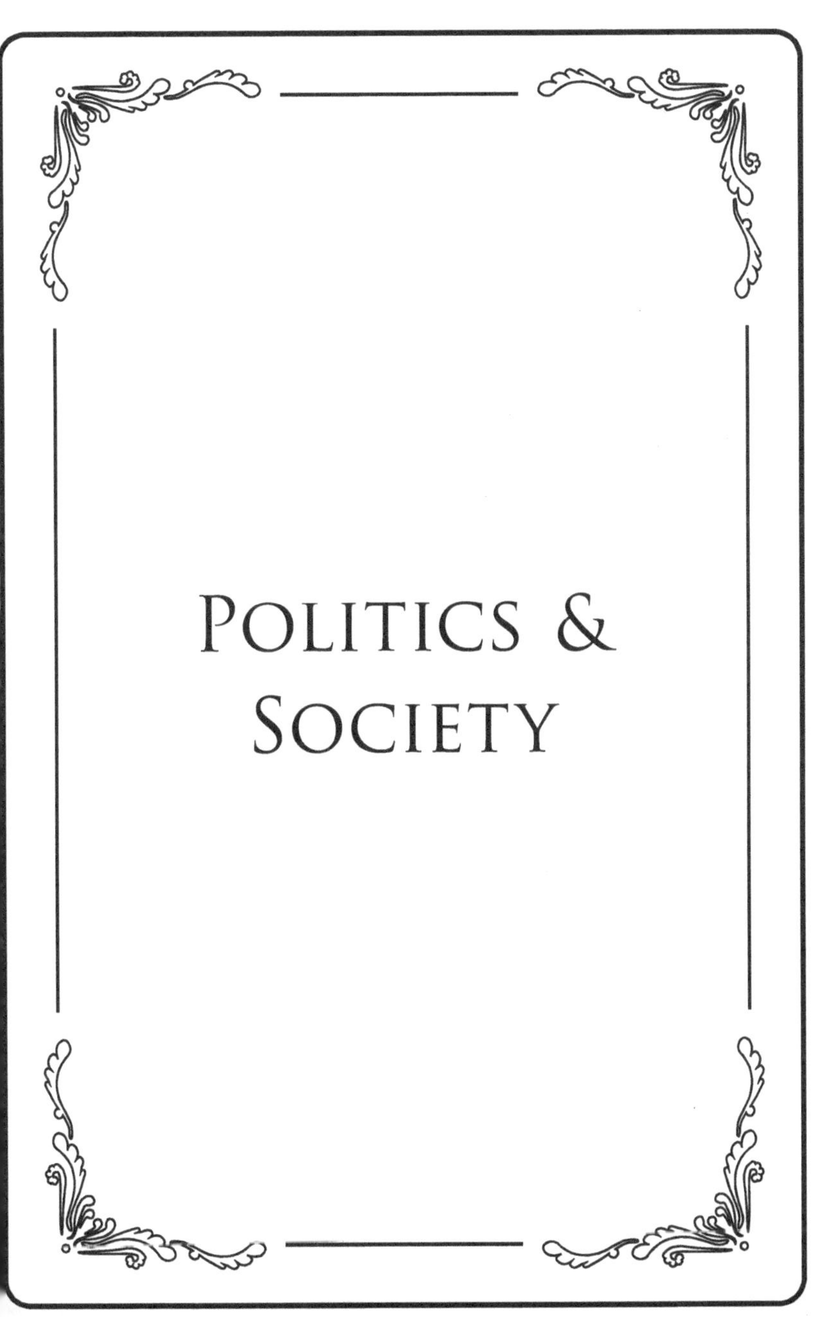

Politics & Society

Twain didn't pull punches when it came to politics, power, or public life. He called things like he saw them whether his opinion was about Congress, patriotism, or the flaws in democracy itself. He believed people could do better, but only if they paid attention and spoke up. These quotes show Twain at his sharpest: honest, skeptical, and never afraid to laugh at the whole system.

Suppose you were an idiot. And suppose you were a member of Congress. But I repeat myself.

—Personal notebooks (1903)

Patriotism is supporting your country all the time, and your government when it deserves it.

—Letter to *The Boston Transcript* (1905)

Lincoln is the only example in history of a man who rose from the lowest ranks of life to the highest without the aid of crime or politics.

—*Mark Twain: A Biography*

If Lincoln had told fewer jokes and made more laws, we'd admire him less—but we'd probably be worse off for it.

—The Mark Twain Project at UC Berkeley

The political and commercial morals of the United States are not merely food for laughter, they are an entire banquet.

—*Autobiography of Mark Twain* (2010)

To lodge all power in one party and keep it there is to insure bad government and the sure and gradual deterioration of the public morals.

—Autobiographical dictation (January 1906)

No man's life, liberty, or property are safe while the legislature is in session.

—Personal notebooks (date unknown)

A statesman is an easy man to make. He only requires a good memory, a bad heart, and a grudge against his kind.

—Often attributed

All kings is mostly rapscallions.

—*The Adventures of Huckleberry Finn* (1885)

The citizen who sees his society moving toward injustice has a duty to resist it.

—Paraphrased

In the beginning of a change, the patriot is a scarce man, brave, hated, and scorned. When his cause succeeds, the timid join him, for then it costs nothing to be a patriot.

—Personal notebooks (1904)

Nothing is so ignorant as a man's vote when he has not heard both sides.

—Personal notebooks (date unknown)

The government is merely a servant—merely a temporary servant; it cannot be its prerogative to determine what is right and what is wrong, and decide who is a patriot and who isn't. Its function is to obey orders, not originate them.

—*The Bible According to Mark Twain* (1995)

The human race is a race of cowards; and I am not only marching in that procession but carrying a banner.

—Personal notebooks (1906)

The trouble with the world is not that people know too little; it's that they know so many things that just aren't so.

—Personal notebooks (date unknown)

Laws control the lesser man... Right conduct controls the greater one.

—Personal notebooks (1903)

It could probably be shown by facts and figures that there is no distinctly native American criminal class except Congress.

—*Following the Equator* (1897)

The only reason why God created man is because he was disappointed with the monkey.

—Personal notebooks (date unknown)

The two most interesting characters of the 19th century are Napoleon and Helen Keller.

—Personal reflection

General (Ulysses S.) Grant's book is a great, unique, and unapproachable literary masterpiece... He was a man who did not say the right thing—he did the right thing.

—Taken from letters and public statements (1885)

RIVER LINE
RIVER LINE

Religion & Philosophy

Twain didn't shy away from big questions. He was skeptical of dogma and deeply curious about faith, morality, and the nature of existence. He used humor to dig at contradictions and encouraged people to think for themselves instead of blindly following the crowd. These quotes capture his sharp take on religion and philosophy—sometimes serious, often funny, and always thought-provoking.

Faith is believing what you know ain't so.

—*Following the Equator* (1897)

Heaven goes by favor. If it went by merit, you would stay out and your dog would go in.

—Personal notebooks (1898)

Man is the religious animal. He is the only religious animal. He is the only animal that has the True Religion—several of them.

—*The Lowest Animal* (1896)

A man is accepted into a church for what he believes and turned out for what he knows.

—Personal notebooks (date unknown)

The two most important days in your life are the day you are born and the day you find out why.

—Often attributed

Go to Heaven for the climate, Hell for the company.

—Personal notebooks (1897)

Religion consists in a set of things which the average man thinks he believes and wishes he was certain of.

—Personal notebooks (1898)

The easy confidence with which I know another man's religion is folly teaches me to suspect that my own is also.

—Personal notebooks (1898)

If there is no God, nothing matters. If there is a God, everything matters.

—Often attributed

I cannot see how a man of any large degree of humorous perception can ever be religious—except he deliberately shut the eyes of his mind and keep them shut by force.

—Personal notebooks (date unknown)

It is by the goodness of God that in our country we have those three unspeakably precious things: freedom of speech, freedom of conscience, and the prudence never to practice either of them.

—*Following the Equator* (1897)

I am not interested to know whether man descended from the ape; I am interested to know whether he has descended from the ape.

—Personal notebooks (date unknown)

If Christ were here now there is one thing he would not be—a Christian.

—Personal notebooks (date unknown)

I don't like to commit myself about heaven and hell—you see, I have friends in both places.

—Personal notebooks (1898)

It is easier to fool people than to convince them they have been fooled.

—Often attributed

The Christian's Bible is a drug store. Its contents remain the same, but the medical practice changes.

—Personal notebooks (1898)

Conscience takes up more room than all the rest of a fellow's insides.

—Personal notebooks (1904)

The Bible has noble poetry in it... and some good morals and a wealth of obscenity, and upwards of a thousand lies.

—*Letters From the Earth* (1940)

When we remember we are all mad, the mysteries disappear and life stands explained.

—Personal notebooks (1898)

You can't reason someone out of something they weren't reasoned into.

—Often attributed

The church is always trying to get other people to reform. It might not be a bad idea to reform itself a little, by way of example.

—Personal notebooks (date unknown)

If you pick up a starving dog and make him prosperous he will not bite you. This is the principal difference between a dog and man.

—Personal notebooks (1898)

The kingdom of Heaven is for those who are poor in spirit, but the taxman prefers those who are rich in gold.

—Paraphrased

RIVER LINE
RIVER LINE

Humor & Writing

Twain's humorous writing made people laugh, but also made them think while they laughed. He had a gift for turning sharp observations into unforgettable one-liners and used humor as a tool for truth. These quotes show his love for language, his sense of timing, and his belief that a well-placed joke can say more than a serious speech.

Keep away from those who try to belittle your ambitions. Small people always do that, but the really great make you believe that you too can become great.

—Personal notebooks (1902)

The difference between the almost right word and the right word is really a large matter—it's the difference between the lightning bug and the lightning.

—Letter to George Bainton (1888)

Humor is mankind's greatest blessing.

—Often attributed

Sanity and happiness are an impossible combination.

—*The Mysterious Stranger* (1916)

Wit is the sudden marriage of ideas which, before their union, were not perceived to have any relation.

—Personal notebooks (date unknown)

I impersonated Lincoln once. I put on a stovepipe hat and stood in thought. The audience wept. Mostly from laughter.

—*Twain in Person* by Louis Budd

Substitute 'damn' every time you're inclined to write 'very'; your editor will delete it and the writing will be just as it should be.

—*Mark Twain's Own Autobiography: The Chapters from the North American Review* (1906)

When you catch an adjective, kill it. No, I don't mean utterly, but kill most of them—then the rest will be valuable.

—Personal notebooks (1880s)

Be respectful to your superiors, if you have any.

—*Advice to Youth* (1882)

I don't give a damn for a man that can only spell a word one way.

—Personal notebooks (1890s)

The humorous story is American, the comic story is English, the witty story is French. The humorous story depends for its effect upon the manner of the telling; the comic story and the witty story upon the matter.

—*How to Tell a Story* (1895)

Good breeding consists in concealing how much we think of ourselves and how little we think of the other person.

—Personal notebooks (date unknown)

Courage is resistance to fear, mastery of fear—not absence of fear.

—*Pudd'nhead Wilson* (1894)

It usually takes me more than three weeks to prepare a good impromptu speech.

—Personal notebooks (1890s)

The right word may be effective, but no word was ever as effective as a rightly timed pause.

—Personal notebooks (1890s)

Never put off till tomorrow what you can do the day after tomorrow just as well.

—Personal notebooks (1880s)

To get the full value of joy you must have someone to divide it with.

—Personal notebooks (1896)

Name the greatest of all inventors. Accident.

—Personal notebooks (1890s)

The reports of my death are greatly exaggerated.

—Letter to Frank Marshall White (1897)

A man who carries a cat by the tail learns something he can learn in no other way.

—Personal notebooks (1894)

Writing is easy. All you have to do is cross out the wrong words.

—Often attributed

Noise proves nothing. Often a hen who has merely laid an egg cackles as if she laid an asteroid.

—*Following the Equator* (1897)

Don't go around saying the world owes you a living. The world owes you nothing. It was here first.

—Personal notebooks (1896)

It ain't what you don't know that gets you into trouble. It's what you know for sure that just ain't so.

—Personal notebooks (1880s)

You can't depend on your eyes when your imagination is out of focus.

—Personal notebooks (1897)

The best way to cheer yourself up is to try to cheer somebody else up.

—Personal notebooks (1902)

When angry, count to four; when very angry, swear.

—*Pudd'nhead Wilson's Calendar* (1894)

Give every day the chance to become the most beautiful day of your life.

—Personal notebooks (1900)

RIVER LINE
RIVER LINE

Life & Death

Twain had a way of talking about life and death that felt honest, funny, and oddly comforting. He didn't avoid the hard stuff, he faced it with clear eyes and a sharp tongue. These quotes offer a glimpse into how he thought about living well, facing mortality, and making the most of the time we have.

The fear of death follows from the fear of life. A man who lives fully is prepared to die at any time.

—Personal notebooks, paraphrased (1896)

Let us endeavor so to live that when we come to die even the undertaker will be sorry.

—*Pudd'nhead Wilson* (1894)

Good friends, good books, and a sleepy conscience: this is the ideal life.

—Personal notebooks (1898)

I do not fear death. I had been dead for billions and billions of years before I was born, and had not suffered the slightest inconvenience from it.

—Often attributed

Do the thing you fear most and the death of fear is certain.

—Personal notebooks (1881)

I was born modest. Not all over, but in spots.

—*Eruption: Hitherto Unpublished Pages About Men and Events* (1940)

Life would be infinitely happier if we could only be born at the age of eighty and gradually approach eighteen.

—Personal notebooks (1903)

It takes your enemy and your friend, working together, to hurt you to the heart; the one to slander you and the other to get the news to you.

—*Following the Equator* (1897)

Life is short. Break the rules, forgive quickly, kiss slowly, love truly, laugh uncontrollably, and never regret anything that made you smile.

—Often attributed

All generalizations are false, including this one.

—Personal notebooks (date unknown)

The lack of money is the root of all evil.

—*More Maxims of Mark* (1927)

Wrinkles should merely indicate where the smiles have been.

—Personal notebooks (1898)

Age is an issue of mind over matter. If you don't mind, it doesn't matter.

—Personal notebooks (1904)

You can't reach old age by another man's road. My habits protect my life but they would assassinate you.

—Personal notebooks (date unknown)

I didn't attend the funeral, but I sent a nice letter saying I approved of it.

—Personal notebooks (1880s)

The average man doesn't like trouble and danger. That is why he is average.

—Personal notebooks (1894)

When your time comes to die, be not like those whose hearts are filled with fear... Sing your death song and die like a hero going home.

—Paraphrased

Honesty is the best policy—when there is money in it.

—Personal notebooks (1894)

Don't part with your illusions. When they are gone you may still exist, but you have ceased to live.

—Personal notebooks (1897)

Forgiveness is the fragrance that the violet sheds on the heel that has crushed it.

—Personal notebooks (1894)

Of all God's creatures there is only one that cannot be made the slave of the lash. That one is the cat.

—Personal notebooks (1894)

Let your sympathies and your compassion be always with the underdog in the fight—this is magnanimity; it is not the seed of heroism, but it is the root of it.

—Personal notebooks (1901)

Oh Death where is thy sting! It has none. But life has.

—Personal notebooks (1894)

The heart is the real fountain of youth.

—Personal notebooks (1902)

You can't make a life over. Society wouldn't let you if you tried.

—Paraphrased

Thunder is good, thunder is impressive; but it is lightning that does the work.

—Personal notebooks (1888)

RIVER LINE
RIVER LINE

Travel & the World

Mark Twain traveled extensively over the course of his life—far more than most people of his time. He was a traveler in every sense of the word: curious, skeptical, and wide-eyed, having visited over 30 countries across North America, Europe, the Middle East, Asia, Africa, and Oceania. He didn't just visit places; he studied them, laughed at them, and learned from them. His journeys shaped his views on humanity, culture, and the absurdities of nationalism. Twain's observations about the world often revealed as much about himself as the places he visited. These quotes reflect a man who saw the world with both wonder and wit.

Travel is fatal to prejudice, bigotry, and narrow-mindedness.

—*The Innocents Abroad* (1869)

Broad, wholesome, charitable views of men and things cannot be acquired by vegetating in one little corner of the earth all one's lifetime.

—*The Innocents Abroad* (1869)

I have found out there ain't no surer way to find out whether you like people or hate them than to travel with them.

—*Tom Sawyer Abroad* (1894)

The gentle reader will never, never know what a consummate ass he can become until he goes abroad.

—*The Innocents Abroad* (1869)

The holy places of the earth are not merely cities or shrines but wherever men walk with open eyes and unclouded hearts.

—*Following the Equator* (1897)

Nothing helps scenery like ham and eggs.

—*Roughing It* (1872)

We wish to learn all the curious, outlandish ways of all the different countries so we can show off and astonish people when we get home.

—*The Innocents Abroad* (1869)

Travel has no longer any charm for me. I have seen all the foreign countries I want to except heaven and hell.

—Letter to *W.D. Howells* (1891)

The mildest, drowsiest man in the world cannot sit down in a first-class railway carriage and travel sixty miles without becoming a quarrelsome lunatic.

—*The Man That Corrupted Hadleyburg* (1900)

It liberates the vandal to travel—you never saw a big man who wasn't more or less vandal at heart.

—*Following the Equator* (1897)

Nothing so liberalizes a man and expands the kindly instincts that nature put in him as travel and contact with many kinds of people.

—Letter to the *San Francisco Alta California* (June 23, 1867)

All that is in the world is worth having, it may be all possessed and yet all left behind.

—Personal notebooks (date unknown)

I would rather feel bad in Idaho than feel good anywhere else.

—Personal notebooks (date unknown)

With all their faults, I love the distance between countries.

—Personal notebooks (date unknown)

There is no unhappiness like the misery of sighting land (and work) again after a cheerful, careless voyage.

—Letter to Will Bowen (1867)

Broad as are the deserts of our knowledge, and narrow as are the conventional paths of travel through them.

—Personal notebooks (date unknown)

A man who speaks two languages is worth two men, and one who travels in two worlds is worth much more.

—Personal notebooks (date unknown)

I was not a young man born to learn, yet travel taught me more than books ever could.

—Personal notebooks (date unknown)

The road is life's grandest teacher, showing us ourselves in every turn.

—Personal notebooks (date unknown)

To do something, say something, see something, before anybody else—these are the things that confer a pleasure compared with which other pleasures are tame and commonplace, other ecstasies cheap and trivial.

—*The Innocents Abroad* (1869)

If I see a truth in a foreign city, I take it home as my own.

—Personal notebooks (date unknown)

Curiosity propelled me farther than fear ever could.

—Personal notebooks (date unknown)

There is something divine in plain living and high thinking on the road.

—Personal notebooks (date unknown)

In America, we hurry—which is well; but when the day's work is done, we go on thinking of losses and gains, we plan for the morrow, we even carry our business cares to bed with us.

—*The Innocents Abroad* (1869)

It is curious—the space-annihilating power of thought.

—*Following the Equator* (1897)

Travel binds us to strangers and separates us from ignorance.

—Personal notebooks (date unknown)

A journey is the journey of the mind as well as the body.

—Personal notebooks (date unknown)

Nothing is so beautiful as the art of traveling far and returning home wiser.

—Personal notebooks (date unknown)

You find your best friend in a traveler, for he understands the wonder of the unknown.

—Personal notebooks (date unknown)

One gets large impressions in boyhood, sometimes, which he has to fight against all his life.

—*The Innocents Abroad* (1869)

Now and then we had a hope that if we lived and were good, God would permit us to be pirates.

—*Life on the Mississippi* (1883)

India has two million gods, and worships them all. In religion, all other countries are paupers; India is the only millionaire.

—*Following the Equator* (1897)

Take the universe as a whole, and it is a very clever conception and quite competently carried out, but I don't think much of this globe as a work of art.

—Often attributed

If travel kills prejudice, it also pins wisdom like a medal on your sleeve.

—Personal notebooks (date unknown)

In our day we don't allow a hundred and thirty years to elapse between glimpses of a marvel.

—*Life on the Mississippi* (1883)

RIVER LINE
RIVER LINE

Freedom & Independence

Mark Twain cherished freedom—not just as a national ideal, but as a personal responsibility. He challenged the status quo, ridiculed injustice, and reminded readers that true liberty begins with the courage to think for yourself. Whether speaking about politics, conscience, or character, Twain believed that independence was more than self-reliance—it was the foundation of integrity. These quotes capture his unwavering belief in freedom of thought, speech, and spirit.

Independence is loyalty to one's best self and principles, and this is often disloyalty to the general idols and fetishes.

—Personal notebooks (1888)

Loyalty to petrified opinion never yet broke a chain or freed a human soul.

—Personal notebooks (1883)

The quality of independence was almost wholly left out of the human race.

—*Autobiography of Mark Twain* (2010)

Whenever you find yourself on the side of the majority, it is time to pause and reflect.

—Personal notebooks (1904)

The soul and substance of what customarily ranks as patriotism is moral cowardice—and always has been.

—Personal notebooks (c. 1900)

The secret of getting ahead is getting started.

—Personal notebooks (1898)

Patriot: the person who can holler the loudest without knowing what he is hollering about.

—*More Maxims of Mark* (1927)

Independence is loyalty to one's own convictions, even when they differ from every voice in the room.

—Personal notebooks (1899)

Morals consist of political morals, commercial morals, ecclesiastical morals, and morals.

—*More Maxims of Mark* (1927)

Irreverence is the champion of liberty and its only sure defense.

—Personal notebooks (1888)

That's the difference between governments and individuals. Governments don't care, individuals do.

—*A Tramp Abroad* (1880)

We are discreet sheep; we wait to see how the drove is going, and then go with the drove.

—*Autobiography of Mark Twain* (2010)

The government is not best which secures mere life and property—there is a more valuable thing—manhood.

—Personal notebooks (c. 1895)

All you need in this life is ignorance and confidence, and then success is sure.

—Letter to Mrs. Foote (1887)

Where every man in a state has a vote, brutal laws are impossible.

—*A Connecticut Yankee in King Arthur's Court* (1889)

To be good is noble; but to show others how to be good is nobler and no trouble.

—*Following the Equator* (1897)

We adore titles and heredities in our hearts and ridicule them with our mouths. This is our democratic privilege.

—*Autobiography of Mark Twain* (2010)

The very ink with which history is written is merely fluid prejudice.

—Personal notebooks (1898)

God created war so that Americans would learn geography.

—Often attributed

Truth stands, even if there be no public support. It is self-sustained.

—Personal notebooks (1900)

We have two opinions: one private, which we are afraid to express; and another one—the one we use—which we force ourselves to wear to please Mrs. Grundy.

—*Autobiography of Mark Twain* (2010)

It's my opinion that everyone I know has morals, though I wouldn't like to ask. But I'd rather teach them than practice them any day.

—Speech given on March 7, 1906

If voting made any difference, they wouldn't let us do it.

—Often attributed

The more you explain it, the more I don't understand it.

—Personal notebooks (1898)

RIVER LINE
RIVER LINE

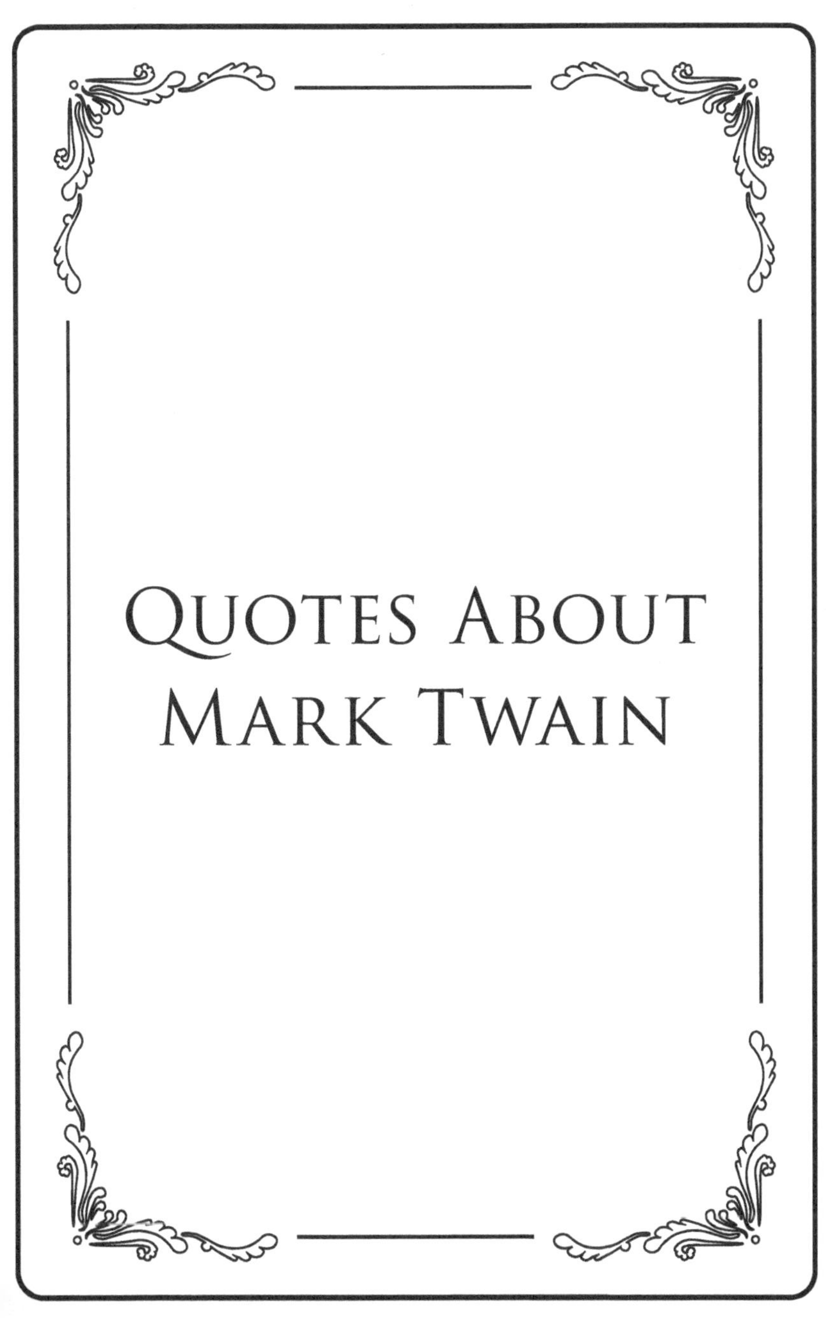

Quotes About Mark Twain

Twain is the rare writer who could dissect human folly while holding up a mirror of sympathy and delight.

—Susan K. Harris

Mark Twain is the true father of American literature.

—William Faulkner

He was, in the best sense, a man of the people. A great moralist, a fierce critic of hypocrisy, and a master of plain speech.

—Gore Vidal

Mark Twain is by far the greatest American writer. I am speaking of him rather as a sociologist than as a humorist.

—George Bernard Shaw

He was not only America's greatest humorist but also a conscience of his generation.

—Ron Powers

Twain gave America its voice and showed us how to laugh at ourselves with grace.

—Ken Burns

Mark Twain is the American Cervantes—more than any other author, he embodies the soul of the country.

—Harold Bloom

He gave to American letters a voice that was lusty and a conscience that was uncompromising.

—Carl Van Doren

All modern American literature comes from one book by Mark Twain called Huckleberry Finn. It's the best book we've had. There was nothing before. There has been nothing as good since.

—Ernest Hemingway

He taught us that humor could be both a weapon and a balm, sharp enough to expose injustice but soft enough to unite us in laughter.

—Maya Angelou

I have been in Eden three days and I saw a King. I knew he was a King the minute I touched him though I had never touched a King before.

—Helen Keller

They were the earlier works of Mark Twain and to them might have been due the miraculous recovery which followed. When I met Mr. Clemens and told him of the experience, I was amazed to see that great man of laughter burst into tears.

—Nikola Tesla, My Inventions (1919)

Emerson, Longfellow, Lowell, Holmes—I knew them all...but Clemens was sole, incomparable, the Lincoln of our literature.

—William Dean Howells

I was introduced to the great Mark Twain, and for the next two hours he spoke and I listened. I had been in the presence of a master, and I was grateful.

—Rudyard Kipling

In *Huckleberry Finn*, Mark Twain wrote a masterpiece of American literature.

—T.S. Eliot

Important Moments in the Life of Mark Twain

Presented here is a timeline highlighting some of the most important moments in Mark Twain's life and beyond:

1835: Samuel Langhorne Clemens is born on November 30 in Florida, Missouri. He is the sixth of seven children in a family plagued by financial instability. Halley's Comet passes Earth during the year of his birth—a fact Twain would later reference as a cosmic bookend to his life.

1839: The Clemens family moves to Hannibal, Missouri, a bustling river town that would later inspire the fictional setting of St. Petersburg in *The Adventures of Tom Sawyer* and *Huckleberry Finn*.

1847: At age 11, Twain's father dies of pneumonia. Forced to leave school, Twain becomes a printer's apprentice, beginning his lifelong relationship with the written word.

1851: Starts contributing humorous sketches and articles to his brother Orion's newspaper, *Hannibal Journal*. His distinctive voice begins to take shape.

1857: Travels to New Orleans and decides to become a steamboat pilot. He begins training under veteran pilot Horace Bixby. The Mississippi River becomes a defining element of his imagination and later his writing.

1859: Earns his steamboat pilot's license. For the next two years, he navigates the Mississippi, adopting the pseudonym "Mark Twain," a riverboat term meaning "two fathoms deep."

1861: The Civil War shuts down Mississippi River traffic. Twain briefly joins a Confederate militia but deserts after two weeks. He heads west to Nevada with his brother Orion, who has been appointed Secretary of the Nevada Territory.

1862: Becomes a journalist in Virginia City, Nevada, working for the *Territorial Enterprise*. It's here that he first uses the pen name "Mark Twain" professionally.

1865: Gains national fame with the publication of "*The Celebrated Jumping Frog of Calaveras County*" in *The New York Saturday Press*. The story captures his blend of satire, tall tale, and regional vernacular.

1867: Travels to Europe and the Middle East aboard the *Quaker City*, an experience he turns into *The Innocents Abroad* (1869). The book is a bestseller and cements his reputation as a witty and skeptical observer of the world.

1870: Marries Olivia "Livy" Langdon, the daughter of a wealthy abolitionist. They settle in Buffalo, New York, and later move to Hartford, Connecticut. Twain begins a period of prolific writing and domestic stability.

1872: Publishes *Roughing It*, a humorous recounting of his travels through the American West. The book is a commercial success.

1874: Moves into the newly completed Hartford home (now the Mark Twain House and Museum). The years spent here are among his most productive.

1876: Releases *The Adventures of Tom Sawyer*, a nostalgic novel rooted in his childhood memories of Hannibal.

1880–1885: Publishes *A Tramp Abroad* (1880), *The Prince and the Pauper* (1881), *Life on the Mississippi* (1883), and *Adventures of Huckleberry Finn* (1885). The latter is considered by many to be the great American novel.

1889: Releases *A Connecticut Yankee in King Arthur's Court*, a biting satire of technology, monarchy, and social progress.

1894: After disastrous investments—including the Paige typesetting machine—Twain files for bankruptcy. He refuses to declare personal insolvency and embarks on a worldwide lecture tour to repay his debts.

1896: His daughter Susy dies of meningitis at age 24, devastating Twain. He is abroad when he receives the news.

1900: Returns permanently to the United States. He is now considered a living legend, widely honored and frequently photographed.

1904: Olivia Langdon Twain dies after a long illness. Twain never fully recovers from the loss.

1907: Receives an honorary doctorate from Oxford University. His reputation abroad, especially in Britain, rivals his fame at home.

1909: His youngest daughter Jean dies suddenly of a heart attack. Twain is grief-stricken. That same year, his close friend Henry H. Rogers also dies.

1910: Mark Twain dies on April 21 in Redding, Connecticut, at age 74—just one day after Halley's Comet reaches its closest point to Earth. He had predicted: *"I came in with Halley's Comet in* 1835. *It is coming again next year, and I expect to go out with it."*

1910: Twain's death is widely mourned. Newspapers across the country refer to him as America's greatest humorist. His funeral is held in New York, and he is buried in Elmira, New York, beside his wife and children.

1940: *Mark Twain in Eruption* is published, collecting posthumous essays, thoughts, and dictations that reflect his late-life observations and wit.

1993: The Kennedy Center establishes the Mark Twain Prize for American Humor, awarded annually to individuals who have had an impact on American society similar to that of Twain through humor. Recipients include Richard Pryor, Carl Reiner, George Carlin, Tina Fey, Dave Chappelle, and Jon Stewart.

2010: On the 100th anniversary of his death, Twain's uncensored autobiography is released as *Autobiography of Mark Twain, Volume 1*, per his instructions. It becomes a bestseller, revealing a rawer, more complex Twain than ever seen before.

Selected Writings & Memorable Moments

Mark Twain was more than a novelist. He was a public intellectual, performer, and cultural critic. His speeches, essays, and autobiographical writings showcase not only his wit but also his evolving views on politics, morality, and society. The following selections represent some of Twain's most memorable moments as a speaker and essayist.

Advice to Youth

(1882)

Delivered with tongue firmly in cheek, this speech to a group of young people offered satirical advice under the guise of moral instruction. Twain encouraged respectful rebellion and cleverness over blind obedience:

Always obey your parents—when they are present. This is the best policy in the long run. Because if you don't, they will make you. Most parents think they know better than you do, and you can generally make more by humoring that superstition than you can by acting on your own better judgment.

Go to bed early, get up early—this is wise. It is also pleasant. Pleasant for those you owe money to.

Never handle firearms carelessly. The sorrow and suffering that has been caused by the accidental discharge of firearms is one of the most distressing features which attend the use of them. For the careless use of firearms has been the basis of more than one good newspaper story, and they often end well, but sometimes they don't. It's best to be cautious.

Now as to lying. You want to be very careful about lying; otherwise you are nearly sure to get caught. Once caught, you can never again be in the eyes of the good and the pure what you were before. You will find that you are pointed at by the finger of scorn, and that sorrow will settle upon your house forever. You will find it easier to live down a new reputation than a bad one. But you need not be discouraged. There is hope for all who look within and seek the higher path.

Do not read books by people who are not at least a hundred years dead. They haven't had time to be properly edited, and time is the best editor there is.

And finally, always remember to be careful about giving advice. It is a responsibility which no man can afford to take lightly. And that's why I'm doing it.

Mark Twain Meets Nikola Tesla

Nikola Tesla grew up in what is now Croatia, a curious and often sickly child surrounded by mystery, imagination, and a deep love of ideas. At one point in his youth, while bedridden and despairing, someone brought him a collection of Mark Twain's short stories.

Years later, Tesla would say that the stories were so captivating they made him "utterly forget [his] hopeless state." It wasn't just distraction; it was healing. He credited Twain's writing with turning his health around and called it a miracle.

"I had hardly recovered from my illness when I read one of Twain's books," he said.

"It made me laugh for the first time in weeks—and laughter really was the best medicine. From that moment, I was on the road to recovery."

Tesla credited Twain's writing—likely *The Innocents Abroad*—with helping him recover from a severe bout of illness as a young man. This personal connection eventually led to their friendship in New York decades later.

In 1888, Tesla and Twain finally met in person. Tesla told him how his books had helped save his life, and Twain, deeply moved, "was amazed to see the great man of laughter burst into tears."

They became close friends. Twain, a lifelong enthusiast of invention and science, spent time in Tesla's New York lab—drawn not just to the machines and electricity, but to the kind of wonder Tesla inspired.

Two icons from very different worlds—one of storytelling, the other of science—connected through something simple and profound: the power of words to save a life.

THE WAR PRAYER

(c. 1905, published posthumously)

A POWERFUL ANTI-WAR parable, The War Prayer was deemed too controversial for publication during Twain's lifetime. In it, a stranger enters a church service where townspeople pray for victory in battle. It is a stunning critique of patriotic blindness and religious hypocrisy. He delivers the unspoken part of their prayer:

It was a time of great and exalting excitement. The country was up in arms, the war was on, in every breast burned the holy fire of patriotism; the drums were beating, the bands playing, the toy pistols popping, the bunched firecrackers hissing and spluttering; on every hand and far down the receding and fading spread of roofs and balconies a fluttering wilderness of flags flashed in the sun; daily the young volunteers marched down the wide avenue gay and fine in their new uniforms, the proud fathers and mothers and sisters and sweethearts cheering them with voices choked with happy emotion as they swung by; nightly the packed mass meetings listened, panting, to patriot oratory which stirred the deepest deeps of their hearts, and which they interrupted at briefest intervals with cyclones of applause, the tears running down their cheeks the while; in the churches the pastors preached devotion to flag and country and invoked the God of Battles beseeching His aid in our good cause in outpourings of fervid eloquence which moved every listener.

It was indeed a glad and gracious time, and the half-dozen rash spirits that ventured to disapprove of the war and cast a doubt upon its righteousness straightway got such a stern and angry warning that for their personal safety's sake they quickly shrank out of sight and offended no more in that way.

Sunday morning came—next day the battalions would leave for the front; the church was filled; the volunteers were there, their young faces alight with martial dreams-visions of the stern advance, the gathering momentum, the rushing charge, the flashing sabers, the flight of the foe, the tumult, the enveloping smoke, the fierce pursuit, the surrender! Then home from the war, bronzed heroes, welcomed, adored, submerged in golden seas of glory!

With the volunteers sat their dear ones, proud, happy, and envying them; their services were recognized; they were welcomed; it was a great day for the church. There was a buzz of excitement which told that something had happened—something out of the ordinary. A stranger had entered the church and was moving with slow and noiseless step up the main aisle, his eyes fixed upon the minister, his long body clothed in a robe that reached to his feet, his head bare, his white hair descending in a frothy cataract to his shoulders, his seamy face unnaturally pale, pale even to ghastliness.

With all eyes following him and wondering, he made his silent way; without pausing he ascended to the preacher's side and stood there waiting. With shut lids the preacher, unconscious of his presence, continued his moving prayer, and at last finished it with the words, uttered in fervent appeal, "Bless our arms, grant us the victory, O Lord our God, Father and Protector of our land and flag!"

The stranger touched his arm, motioned him to step aside—which the startled minister did—and took his place. During some moments he surveyed the spellbound audience with solemn eyes, in which burned an uncanny light; then in a deep voice he said:

"I come from the Throne, bearing a message from Almighty God!"

The words smote the house with a shock; if the stranger perceived it he gave no attention. He has heard the prayer of His servant your shepherd and will grant it if such shall be your desire after I, His messenger, shall have explained to you its import—that is to say, its full import. For it is like many of the prayers of men, in that it asks for more than he who utters it is aware of—except he pause and think.

God's servant and yours has prayed his prayer. Has he paused and taken thought? Is it one prayer? No, it is two—one uttered, the other not. Both have reached the ear of the God of Battles. He is the source of both."

Then came the prayer we already know:

O Lord our God, help us to tear their soldiers to bloody shreds with our shells..."

Then he paused, and his voice softened:

Ye have prayed it; if ye still desire it, speak! The messenger of the Most High waits."

It was believed afterward that the man was a lunatic, because there was no sense in what he said.

REFLECTIONS ON MARK TWAIN

As you have journeyed through the wit and wisdom of Mark Twain, I hope these quotes have brought a smile, sparked reflection, and maybe even challenged you to see things differently. Twain had a way of holding up a mirror—sometimes sharp, sometimes generous—and reminding us not to take life too seriously.

He believed in humor as a way to tell the truth, and in honesty as something worth striving for even when it's uncomfortable.

His voice still rings clear more than a century later because he wasn't just clever—he was *real.*

May these words stay with you in the quiet moments, the hard decisions, and the times you need a laugh. And may they encourage you to think for yourself, speak plainly, and live with courage and curiosity.

For more writings, books, and reflections, visit travishellstrom.com. You'll find other collections and ideas there—just like this one—made to help you slow down, ask better questions, and enjoy the journey.